Waiting in Joy

AN ADVENT JOURNEY

JOHN SCALLY

First published in 2018 by Messenger Publications

Cover image: graphic-line/ Shutterstock

ISBN 978 1 788120 09 8

Sir John Betjeman 'Christmas' from
A Few Late Chrysanthemums © John Murray

Designed by Messenger Publications Design Department
Typeset in Palatino and Trajan
Printed by Johnswood Press Ltd

Messenger Publications,
37 Lower Leeson Street, Dublin D02 W938
www.messenger.ie

DEDICATION

To Raphael Gallagher

A Wonderful Teacher and a Compassionate Man

Introduction

*'The words that I have spoken are spirit
and they are life.' (Jn 6:63)*

This book is written for those who are more concerned with the Christmas Presence than those who simply want to get loads of Christmas presents. Most of us love Christmas, but sometimes we are so busy that we neglect to prepare for the true meaning of this most magical season which pulsates with Good News. This book sets out to challenge this tendency. We are often so preoccupied with the hustle and bustle of Christmas preparations that we neglect to take time to prepare for the coming of that baby who would change the course of history and turn the world on its head.

Using pieces from the Scriptures, thoughtful and interesting reflections and seasonal prayers the aim of this book is to promote self-questioning, to challenge and integrate faith and life in the modern world, while mindful of the richness of the Christian tradition and the basic yearnings of our hearts as we prepare to welcome the greatest news of all.

The great mystic St John of the Cross wrote: 'Come, O beautiful soul. Know, now, that your desired beloved lives hidden within your heart.' This book is written for all those who are preparing for Christmas by making such a journey of the heart this Advent.

Week One

Sunday

'He will yield authority over the nations
and adjudicate between many peoples;
these will hammer their swords into ploughshares,
their spears into sickles.' (Is 12:8)

Reflection: The long and winding road

Karl Rahner almost ruined my life. As a young theology student the complexity of his thought and the density of his language was a diet too rich for my teenage sensibilities. The great Jesuit's apparently impenetrable musings on the Trinity in particular drove me to despair. With advancing years though my antipathy for the greatest theologian of the last century has mellowed. In fact I now really appreciate his writings on revelation. He distinguishes between the definitive Revelation in Jesus Christ and the Bible on the one hand and those accidental revelations that come to us among the mundane rituals of everyday life on the other.

Patrick Kavanagh had a keen awareness of this when he spoke of finding God in the 'bits and pieces of everyday'. His poem 'Advent' captures this insight brilliantly: 'And Christ comes with a January flower.'

Rahner summed up Christmas evocatively as, 'a time when grace is the air'. He saw Advent as a journey into grace – a time for us to slow down and reflect and let the presence of a loving God seep through our lives.

Rahner also saw Advent as a journey into Good News – God's love for us – God's hope, life, wisdom, truth and healing. Such a journey is made in silence, to embrace a voice that speaks without words, a quiet that is loud with conviction, the calm at the centre of a storm. For Rahner Advent is the time when God issues a special gold-plated invitation for us to journey into the divine presence.

At every point in the story of the Jewish people and of the birth of Christianity, journeys play a major role. The journey of Moses and his people from Egypt through the wilderness to safety were key events in the history of Israel. For the people of Israel these journeys were also a central feature of their experience of God.

It was as they journeyed that they discovered that God was accompanying them. It was as they travelled that they came to know God and to understand their nature as the people of God.

Journeys were also central to the life of Jesus. The frequent journeys around Galilee, the wandering of the wilderness, the journey to Jerusalem, enabled Jesus to explain the nature of the Kingdom of God and what it means to be a Christian.

The parable of Good Samaritan (Lk 10:30–37) is one example. 'Anyone who does not take his cross and follow in my footsteps' (Mt 10:38). These stories and sayings of Jesus all indicate that to be a Christian involves moving from one set of values to another, and from one way of acting to another.

The Christian story is a pilgrimage, a journey of discovery, towards union with God.

Advent is a time for us to prepare for the coming of Christ, an ideal opportunity for us to take the time to journey into the mystery of God.

The liturgical year begins on the first Sunday of Advent. This day represents a new beginning in the Christian pilgrimage. The birth of Jesus offered a new beginning to the world, a new way of life. In this special season let us take up Jesus' invitation to make a new beginning.

PRAYER
O Father of mercy,
give me strength to overcome my weakness
and the patience to endure my pains.
Inspire me to be humble,
lessen my foolish fears.
Give me an appreciation of what is worthy,
and strengthen my love of You and others

❀ ❀ ❀

MONDAY

'Open to me the gates of holiness:
I will enter and give thanks.
This is the Lord's own gate
where the just may enter.
I will thank for you have given answer
and you are my saviour.' (Ps 117:19–21)

Reflection: All you need is love
At school an important part of our preparation for the season was the making of Christmas cards. Part of this reason was economic – we could give cards to family members and relatives without incurring any expense. There was

also a religious reason; at least half our cards had to have a nativity scene drawn on the cover. As a concession we were also allowed to put non-religious Christmas scenes on some of the cards. However, I suspect the main reason for this activity was that it kept us quiet for hours and hours. There was a bag of sweets for the person with the best card, which provided a definite incentive for us all to do our very best at a time when we were at our most giddy. We were all 'encouraged' to incorporate an inspirational or religious message. The message 'suggested' for me was St John of the Cross' poem 'The Incarnation':

> *Then He called*
> *The archangel Gabriel*
> *And sent him to*
> *The Virgin Mary*

> *At whose consent*
> *The mystery was wrought*
> *In whom the Trinity*
> *Clothed the Word with flesh*

> *And though three work this*
> *It is wrought in the one;*
> *And the Word lived incarnate*
> *In the womb of Mary.*

> *And He who had only a father*
> *Now had a Mother too,*
> *But she was not like others*
> *Who conceive by man.*

From her own flesh
He received His flesh
So he is called
Son of God and of man.
(The Poetry of John of the Cross translated by David
Lewis 1814–1895)

As I got older I developed a great affection for St John of the Cross, the man and the poet, but as an eight year-old, the finer theological points of this poem escaped me. However, the fact that I can still quote from it suggests that there may have been a positive pedagogical value to the exercise after all.

Now when I read this poem I understand that it is through love alone that we please God and our main challenge is to acquire it. Jesus came on earth to love and be loved – to win love for our love. The Christian life is an exchange of love – the love we receive and the love we give God.

The season of Advent is a golden opportunity for each one of us to commit ourselves to this exchange of love. Each day of Advent is an opportunity to learn something about love and to grow ever more in love.

PRAYER
Lord,
Thank you for my life today.
This Advent give me the key to the door of truth,
so that I may discover myself each day,
a better person in every way.

❋ ❋ ❋

TUESDAY

'And behold the Lord passed by, and a great and strong
wind rent the mountains, and broke in pieces the rocks
before the Lord, but the Lord was not in the wind, and
after the end an earthquake, and after the earthquake a
fire, and after the fire a still small voice.'
(1 Kgs 19:11–12)

Reflection: The Shy God
The above piece from the Book of Kings provides an illu-
minating insight into God's revelatory activity: God came
not in a whirlwind but in a still small voice.

Such a model allows us to see God present in the nature
of all things and puts the onus on us to discern this presence. God's actions are hidden, because they are constant
and because God acts within everything.

Just as we are never conscious of air, because God's presence is always around us, we never notice it. The journey
of faith is a gift of a loving God who takes the first step
and waits patiently, silently, almost shyly for the human
response.

Life is a vocation, a call to seek this shy God.

This shy God did not come into the world with bells and
thunder. When I was a young boy I sought God by looking
up – trying to see if I could find God through some break
in the sky. Today when I look for God I look down not up
because I find God in small things. As Pope Francis has
said we find the extraordinary in the ordinary.

The search for God this Advent requires us to look
down. In doing so we follow the example of God. This shy
God chose to become among us not in a palace or in a busy

street but to become small and be born in a manger in the form of a helpless baby.

Advent is a time to remind ourselves of the many contradictions at the heart of our faith. This most powerful presence chose to be manifest in powerlessness.

As we prepare to celebrate the moment the Word became flesh our faith needs deepening. Ours is a faith that sincerely accepts the darkness surrounding the search for more light. Consequently Advent is a time of loving adoration, a true act of supernatural hope and of loving surrender to this shy God.

This shy God reminds us this Advent that life is about relationships not about things. The greatest joy comes from good relationships – the greatest sorrow and suffering come not from loss of job or property but from broken and betrayed relationships. All relationships of love are rooted in the love this shy God has for all of us.

PRAYER

Lord,
you were born in pain and love,
given to us on earth for a short time only,
before you left us again in love and pain.
One day you will come to us again.
Help us to be worthy of you.
Lead us into your truth,
to beauty and to the secret of living the good life.

❄ ❄ ❄

WEDNESDAY

*'Whether you turn to right or left, your ears will hear
these words behind you, "This is the way, follow it".
He will send rain for the seed you sow in the ground,
and the bread that the ground provides will be rich and
nourishing.' (Is 30:23)*

Reflection: On the run

It is easy to have a very romantic view of the Christmas story. This is the time of year when we start to buy our Christmas cards and many perpetuate a sentimental notion of Christmas – one that often bears little or no relation to the original Christmas story.

Advent is a time to step back from the 'Disneyisation' of Christmas and remember the original cast of characters. Few are more interesting or compelling in this perspective than Mary.

Growing up on a farm, I knew that the nativity scene could not possibly have been the romantic, sweet-smelling, clean event portrayed on so many Christmas cards. Despite the great advances in farming methods and buildings I had never been in a stable that was fit for a baby to be born. I could imagine the smells, the draughts, and the scatterings of farmyard manure. This really brought home to me the hardships and discomfort of the first Christmas.

I felt a particular sympathy for Mary. I felt a kinship with her because we were both born into a very rigid and traditional society. Such a close-knit community had advantages and disadvantages. The major disadvantage was that there was no way of maintaining one's privacy. News of her 'shame' must have been music to the ears of all the gossips. I imagined how painful it must have been for Mary to know that everyone was talking about her. In the Jewish society of that time, doing the right thing was less important than being seen to do the right thing. For this reason I was able to make connections between the first Christmas story and my own.

I understood how painful and distressing it must have been for Mary to see Joseph, the man to whom she was betrothed, become another innocent victim of this gossip as well. I knew the story of the nativity was anything but a fairy tale. Although few things in life are more joyful than childbirth the immediate days and weeks before the birth were very stressful and uncomfortable. I assumed it must have been even worse for a first-time mother. I could only imagine what it must have been like for Mary to have set off on a long journey on the back of a donkey. Having often travelled on the back of a donkey myself I had a good inkling as to what was involved for her.

Worse was to follow. There was no place where she could have her baby even in meagre comfort. Then after having her baby she had to flee the stable because somebody wanted to kill her child.

Advent is a clarion call for us to remember the manner of God's birth. We should never forget that Jesus is both the son of God and the son of woman.

PRAYER

Mary,
Inspire me to have a faith like yours
a willingness to say yes to God,
when it is more convenient to go my own way.
As you carried the baby inside you
there must have been moments of discomfort
but you never wavered.
Help me to find strength like yours.

❈ ❈ ❈

THURSDAY

*'He does not judge by appearances,
he gives no verdict on hearsay.' (Is 11:4)*

Reflection: Try a Little Tenderness

Sometimes Jack found it hard to sleep. His problems were compounded one night when, in his semi-conscious slumber, he became aware of an insistent sound of scraping and scratching. Eventually he lit his bedside candle. There was a silence, but, when he blew out his candle, the irritating noise resumed, and penetrated the stillness of the night. 'It must be a mouse' thought Jack to himself. He got up again and retrieved his old mousetrap from its home in an old shoebox and delicately secured a morsel of cheese on its spike. After leaving the trap where he thought the noise of the scratching was he climbed into bed. He lay very still, determined not to fall asleep, but slowly his eyes got heavier and he drifted towards sleep.

The sudden, unmistakable snap of the trap jerked him out of his dozing. He sat up not quite sure, for a second, or two, where he was. Then he heard a pained squealing from the corner of his room. He groped in the dark for the matches to light his candle and dragged himself out of his bed. The rheumatism which so often crippled him was playing up again in the cold weather. There in the corner was the mouse, its tail firmly caught in the trap. It was vigorously, vainly tugging at its tormentor, but it wouldn't let go.

'Hah, hah you little devil you. I have you now you cheeky little so and so', shouted Jack in triumph. The mouse looked up at him. Its tiny black, beady eyes screamed one emotion – fear. Jack stopped dead in his tracks. He knew that feeling. His mind flashed back over fifty years.

Craving excitement he had enlisted in the British army in 1940 and found himself deployed in the desert in North Africa. Jack's American Sherman tank was isolated and attacked by the Germans. As he attempted to escape Jack was shot in the leg. A young German soldier was dispatched to finish him off.

The throb of military vehicles was deafening. As the blood oozed from his leg Jack lunged in manic desperation for his rifle. A sudden, despairing sickness ran through him as he felt the barrel of a gun on the back of his head. He raised his hands slowly. He tried to pray but his mouth seemed in a vice-grip and he could not will speech. Expecting a bullet to end his life at any second he ever so slowly began to turn his head. The German could have been no more than seventeen. Jack was not going to beg:

'Why don't you get it over with and finish me off sonny? You're just wasting your time and mine. For God's sake just finish it.'

His executor seemed almost more afraid than he was

17

– paralysed by indecision. He pulled back his gun. Jack –raced himself and closed his eyes. To his astonishment when he opened his eyes a few moments later the German soldier was running away.

Jack lay emotionally exhausted in the searing heat unable to make the effort to get back to camp. A few hours later he was rescued by his colleagues . . .

Reality rudely reasserted itself and obliterated Jack's reminiscences, and he was dragged back to the present by the sound of the mouse tussling with the trap. Watching the mouse dragging the implacable contraption with his tail jolted Jack into action. He tenderly took the mousetrap in his hand and set the mouse free.

Memory is central to all our lives.

Advent challenges us to remember who we really are as Christians.

Who are you?

PRAYER
Lord,
lead me to you,
live in my words,
live in my thoughts,
live in my actions,
live in my life.

✿ ✿ ✿

FRIDAY

'In due course John the Baptist appeared; he preached
in the wilderness of Judea and this was his message:
Repent, for the kingdom of heaven
is close at hand.' (Mt 3:1)

Reflection: Two In One

Head said: 'I am full of bright ideas'.

Heart said: 'I am full of tenderness and passion'.

Head said: 'I am reason. I am order. I am the lynchpin which holds everything together'.

Heart said: 'I am feeling. I am mystery. I am the creative energy which sparks wonder and authentic life'.

Then Head and Heart began to squabble. Head said: 'You are easily swayed and misled. You live in a world without order'.

Heart replied: 'You are dispassionate and detached. You don't live. You just exist'.

So Head and Heart went to God and asked if they could be split up. God laughed at them and said: 'You two belong together. Apart you are worthless. Head you are the container. Heart, you are the contents. The container without the contents is as useless as an empty vessel, all sham and no substance. The contents without the container will scatter to the ends of the earth, and blow into the empty wind. It's not possible for you to live apart and have productive lives.'

Head and Heart were puzzled: 'But we are total opposites. How can we find harmony?' God said: 'Draw close and embrace like lovers. Protect each other. Look out for each other. Help each other to be equal partners. Then you will join together as one and I promise you something fantastic and wonderful will happen.'

At this Head and Heart asked in unison: 'What?'

God simply smiled and said: 'Wait and see.'

I like to think of Advent as the season of the head and Christmas as the season of the heart. Advent is a time of self-questioning, that challenges us to integrate faith and life in the modern world. The build-up to Christmas is always frenetic with presents to be bought and many cards to be written. So why do I believe the season of Advent is important? I need to take the time to remember every Advent a wonderful message – God has transformed our brokenness by taking it on and waits for us to grow ever more into the image and likeness of the divine.

As children we did not go in for the Advent calendar. My mother wanted us to embrace the season. Every year she would buy us a box of lemon sweets at the start of December and show where she was putting them up on the very top of the wardrobe where they would be out of sight and out of our reach. However, she stressed they would be waiting for us there to be opened on Christmas morning. It was a valuable lesson about the meaning of Advent.

It is a time of waiting.

It is a time of waiting for God.

It is a time of waiting for perfect love.

It is a time of waiting to become our true selves.

It is a time to remember that everything that is worthwhile is worth waiting for.

PRAYER

Lord,
You offered your life as Good News
I thank you for that.
The world needs good news now more than ever.
Never let me forget who I am.
Help me this Advent renew my dedication to you,
so that my life may be a celebration of your love.

✿ ✿ ✿

SATURDAY

*'The Day of the Lord will come like a thief, and then
with a roar the sky will vanish, the elements will catch
fire and fall apart, the earth and all that it contains
will be burnt up. . . . What we are waiting for is what
he promised: the new heavens and the new earth, the
place where righteousness will be at home. So then,
my friends, while you are waiting, do your best to live
lives without spot or stain so that you will find peace.'*
(Lk 3: 12–14)

Reflection: Silent Night

My first teacher, Mrs McDonnell, was not prone to fine
words or flights of fancy, but she did not need to be because she spoke louder and more effectively by her actions.

I can still remember her teaching us the nativity. The
gospel was taken from St Luke and began: 'In the sixth
month, the angel Gabriel was sent from God to the city
of Galilee named Nazareth to a virgin betrothed to a man
named Joseph' (Lk 2:1–2).

We also read the nativity narratives story of how the angel spoke to the shepherds on the hillside and reported that: 'they went in haste and found Mary and Joseph'. Looking back now I wonder if that was the first Christmas rush!

That year Mrs McDonnell also taught me my two favourite Christmas stories. The first was about a song. In 1818, a roving band of actors was performing in towns throughout the Austrian Alps. In December they arrived at Oberndorf, a village near Salzburg where they were to re-enact the story of Christ's birth in the small Church of St Nicholas. Sadly, the church organ was not working and would not be repaired before Christmas. As the church organ was out of commission, the actors presented their Christmas drama in a private home. That Christmas presentation of the events in the first chapters of Matthew and Luke put pastor Josef Mohr in a reflective mood. Instead of walking straight home that night, Mohr took a longer way home. The longer path took him up over a hill overlooking the village. From that hilltop, Mohr looked down on the peaceful snow-covered village. He feasted his eyes on the glowing Christmas-card-like scene. He suddenly remembered a poem he had written a couple of years before. That poem was about the night when angels heralded the birth of the long-awaited Messiah to shepherds on a hillside. Mohr decided those words might make a good carol for his congregation the following evening at their Christmas eve service but he did not have any music to which that poem could be sung. So, the next day he went to see the church organist, Franz Xavier Gruber. By that evening, Gruber had managed to compose a musical setting for the poem. They now had a Christmas carol that could be sung without that organ. It was 'Stille Nacht' or 'Silent Night'.

The second was the story of how Christmas stopped a war when the fierce and bloody First World War came to a halt on the day of Christ's birth in one corner of the western front. The Germans waved and called out speaking in simple French, holding out cigars they asked for English jam in return. 'Stille Nacht' and 'Silent Night' rang out on different sides. The words were different but the sentiments remained the same. A football was produced and a game of soccer took place. Music and sport, two of the languages which could have united the participants at the Tower of Babel. For a moment at least compassion carried more power than cruelty.

In Advent God whispers gently into our ears with loving calls for each of us to become vessels of compassion. How will we answer?

PRAYER

Lord,
Open my mouth
so that I can speak your words more fearlessly
Open my eyes
so that I can see you more clearly.
Open my heart
so that I can love you more dearly.

❊ ❊ ❊

SUNDAY

*'Someone is following me, someone is more powerful
than I am, and I am not fit to kneel down and undo the
strap of his sandals. I have baptised you with water,
but he will baptise you with the Holy Spirit.'*
(Mk 1:8)

Reflection: Little Things Mean A Lot

Once a great king was preparing to go to war and he sent his servant to the blacksmith to be certain his horse was ready. The blacksmith told the groom he had no iron to shoe the horse. The king would have to wait. The groom said this was not on and he would make do with what he had. The blacksmith tried his best, but he had not enough iron to correctly fasten the fourth shoe.

The battle began in earnest. The king was leading his troops from the front when his horse's shoe fell off. The horse stumbled and rolled over. The king was thrown to the ground. His men deserted him when they saw his plight. The king was captured and the battle was lost. And all because of a missing nail! The great Irish poet William Butler Yeats was going home from work one cold winter's evening. Having failed to find a coat hanger that morning, he had casually thrown his overcoat at the foot of the Abbey Stage. However, when he went back for it that evening, a little kitten had snuggled up inside the coat and was now fast asleep. Rather than disturb the kitten it is said that Yeats went backstage and got a scissors and cut the section of his coat that was sheltering the kitten and headed out in the cold night air with a big hole in his coat!

Little things do mean a lot. As we prepare for Christmas

we remember that God has showered us with gifts – none more so than when he sent his only Son. Those gifts come with a challenge. Christianity is not about occasional gestures of charity but about going the extra mile, about making choices which involve inconvenience, discomfort and pain. The force of love, of unexpected and invigorating vitality is what animates Christians. Only true love carries memorial weight, regenerates moments of tenderness, of unions of spirit. Such a love is never encountered in stony walls or architectural masterpieces rising to an impassive sky. The Christian's primary obligation is not to build memorials to the dead but to give food to the living. Advent is a timely reminder that the secret of life is that only in love for the living is the spirit praised forever.

Few of us have the power to change the world but this Advent we can all do something, albeit something small, to improve life for our neighbour. Today the depth of our commitment to Christ is gauged by the extent to which we love our neighbour. After all, if all we think about is number one, we are not going to add up to very much.

PRAYER
Lord,
My heart swells with a joy,
I want to share with everyone,
the story of our greatness and goodness.
I am incapable of communicating
a message that is so awesome.
Glory to you, O Lord in this season of expectation,
help me to be an agent of your glory.

❄ ❄ ❄

WEEK TWO

MONDAY

*'And the forests and every fragrant tree will provide
shade for Israel at the command of God; for God will
guide Israel in joy by the light of his glory with his
mercy and integrity for escort.'*
(Bar 5:9)

Reflection: Straight from the Heart

The abbot was distressed. A few days ago his problem
seemed resolved. The problem had been dragging on now
for a number of years. All the monks were getting very
old and although they were still able to do their chores,
their voices were well past their best and the community
singing had suffered terribly. The main problem was of
course, Br Seán, who sang, if such a word could be used,
in a high-pitched squeaky voice, doing violence to the ears
of those unlucky enough to be in his immediate vicinity.

Then, one day, as if by a miracle, a young man joined
the community who had the voice of an angel. When he
sang solo, everyone was enthralled by the sheer beauty of
his voice; time just seemed to stand still. His solo singing
brought a dramatic improvement to community worship,
but not even he could cover up for Br Seán.

Now the abbot faced a new problem. The local bishop
had unexpectedly sent a message to say he would be

starting a three day visit to the community. How could the abbot possibly subject the bishop to Br Seán's singing? There was only one course of action, the abbot decided to instruct Br Seán not to sing while the bishop was visiting. The abbot didn't want to hurt Br Seán's feelings, but pleasing the bishop was more important than the pride of a simple monk.

The next day Br Seán sat quietly in the back of the chapel. The singing went beautifully. The bishop was loud in his praise of the quality of the singing. The abbot went to bed, a happy man that night. He smiled contentedly, thinking that the day couldn't have gone any better. But that night an angel came to visit the abbot. 'What happened to the singing tonight? We didn't enjoy it as much as normal. We particularly missed Br Seán's singing. He sings the Lord's praises so beautifully.'

The abbot couldn't believe his ears. 'Br Seán is a terrible singer. He has a voice like a growling dog. How could you possibly enjoy his singing.'

'Ah, you don't understand,' said the angel, 'You see in heaven, we listen to the heart.'

Advent is a time of challenge. It compels us to think anew about what it is that really matters and equally what does not matter. Each of us have many voices racing around in our heads. The challenge of Advent is to remember that we only see with the heart. What is essential is invisible to the eye.

PRAYER

Lord,
You healed the sick,
you fed the hungry,
you gave sight to the blind,
you brought comfort to the lonely,
you befriended the outcast,
you loved the unlovable.
We rejoice in your love.

✿ ✿ ✿

TUESDAY

*'The virgin will conceive and give birth to a son and
they will call him Emmanuel.' (Mt 1:24)*

Reflection: In the Name of the Son

'And they called him Emmanuel'.

From the very beginning Christians thought, spoke and
acted not in their own name, but in the name of the Lord.
Jesus called the disciples to live in his name, to pray in his
name (Jn 15:10), to meet in his name (Mt 18:20), to welcome little children in his name (Mt 18:5) to cast out devils
in his name (Mk 9:38), to work miracles in his name (Mk
9:39) and to preach repentance to all nations in his name
(Lk 24:47).

To live in the name of the Lord is to partake in an intimately personal relationship. To think, speak and act in
the name of the Lord means that the divine name is the
sacred space by which Christians can hear with their ears,
see with their own eyes and touch with their own hands
the Word who is life and the subject of their witness (1 Jn:

I). The name is a dwelling place, the ideal retreat to listen to Christ and receive the Word which is to be spoken. The name is the setting where the future meets the present. Only when the name is the true centre can we be free to heal the sick because it is only then that is possible to understand that the love of God and the love of neighbour cannot be separated.

A Christian is one who lives in communion with Jesus, and through him with the Trinitarian God. Being in touch with numerous people but out of touch with the Lord -- involved in a commendable and worthy apostolate but divorced from divine 'affairs' is anathema. To be true to the gospel vision it is necessary to keep one's eyes on the Lord, to remain attentive to his will and to listen with care to his voice (Lk 10:42). Only with, in and through Jesus Christ can the apostolate bear fruit, as we live in ongoing communion with the one who calls us out to witness in his name.

The Christian is first and foremost a person of prayer. Without prayer, the Christian life easily descends to a mere busy life in which a person's need for respect or affection dominates actions and being busy becomes a badge of honour – an end in itself. It is not necessarily true that absence makes the heart grow fonder. As many a ruined romance has demonstrated absence may cause the heart to wander. The parallel for prayer life does not need to be laboured.

While the first Christians in many cases heroically gave all of themselves to the apostolate they never deluded themselves that their work was their prayer. This is as crucial an insight for the Christian life now as it was then.

For other religions 'the call to prayer' is at the heart of

their faith. Advent is a forceful reminder that the call to prayer is central to our lives also.

PRAYER

Lord,
Give me strength in my moments of crisis
so that I may find the will to go on.
Help me to be a vehicle
which sings your praise to others.
May I be in you
and you in me.
I ask this in your name.

✿ ✿ ✿

WEDNESDAY

'For I was a stranger and you gave me welcome,
I was naked and you gave me clothes,
I was hungry and thirsty and you gave me food and drink,
I was in pain and you gave me comfort.' (Mt 25)

Reflection: Who We Are

Sarah's dinner was a very simple one of eggs, hot cocoa, biscuits and butter. Tears came to her eyes, not for the first time that day, as she thought of her late husband. How quickly those marvellous months melted away when they were so happily married.

Sarah woke from her afternoon slumber with a start. A crashing sound boomed through the air. Somebody was knocking at the door. Sarah's heartbeat accelerated; nobody ever came to see her any more, but last night she had the strangest dream that the Lord himself would visit her on her birthday. Sarah herself had been born on this day seventy years ago. Her face fell when she saw a shabby old beggar standing on the doorstep. 'What a foolish old woman I am becoming' she thought to herself. The stranger's clothes were ragged and threadbare and his shoes were badly worn out. Sarah brought him inside, sat him beside the fire, gave him a mug of steaming tea and went off to look for her late husband's old coat and boots. They fitted the stranger perfectly. With tears in his eyes the old man bade farewell. Sarah started to tidy up.

Within moments, through the clear frosty air, there came a faint knock. This time it was a bent old woman. She had curly white hair, a very haggard face, brown eyes and a sad smile. 'Could you give me some money and God bless you ma'am?' Sarah shook her head regretfully. 'Come in anyway!' The old woman sat beside the fire while Sarah made her some hot tomato soup and gave her two slices of brown bread. The woman looked at the 'feast' with delight and savoured every mouthful. Then after a short chat she left warm and contented. Sarah thought how strange it was that she should be visited by two strangers in such a remote place. An hour and a half later there was another knock. This time it was a beautiful, slim, pale-faced young woman. 'I'm really sorry to trouble you but would you mind if I came in and sat down for a few minutes because I think I have twisted my ankle'. Sarah bathed the ankle and bandaged it expertly to prevent any swelling. The young woman thanked her sincerely and Sarah walked her to the door and they exchanged goodbyes.

Sarah shut the door and went back inside. What an extraordinary day it had been! Suddenly she walked over to the mantelpiece and picked up to her old Bible. It was covered in a sheet of dust. After a short search she found the lines she was looking for in Matthew 25.

A sudden twinkle came back into Sarah's eyes. Dreams come true after all!

A key part of Advent is to become ever more attentive to the presence of Jesus in bruised, battered or broken people.

PRAYER

Open our ears to hear your wisdom,
open our eyes to see your innocence.
Don't let us take you for granted.
Give us the courage to give you the key
to our sacred hearts
and not be afraid to show you who we are.

✿ ✿ ✿

THURSDAY

'The Lord is good to all and has compassion on all he has made.' (Ps 145:9)

Reflection: Act Socially

Advent is the season of the needy. Poverty has not been created by God. We are the ones who have created poverty. Before God, we are all poor.

Jesus is the one we take care of, visit, clothe, feed and comfort every time we do to the poorest of the poor, to the sick, to the dying, to the lepers and to the ones who suffer from AIDS.

Every Advent we remember those who are bruised and broken, melancholic or moody. We pray for those who in a peculiar way both look forward to the season of good cheer and dread it and for those who are impatient for the magic that never comes for them but which all the preparations promise. Christmas is above all for them a time to be lonely. In times of emigration we remember those with families scattered all over the world, England, Australia, America and Canada. Some feel exile, home-sickness, longing and hoped-for returns that would never materialise, and are trapped in a prison of memories. Their pain is the piercing grief of never being able to return to the way things used to be.

We also recall the elderly people who live alone and whose loneliness become more intense with each passing Christmas. Every year their longing for warmth and af-fection becomes more desperate. For some, Christmas is little more than a painful reminder of missed chances for lasting happiness.

One of the great tragedies of life today is that so many people are dying from a lack of love – in a world where al-most everyone wants to love. Sadly we are unable to pour out love upon people who are starving for love. The lack of love is the great hunger of today.

Advent is a reminder that Jesus came to us with loving hands. He touched so many people in need during his thirty-three years on earth. His touch was warm and gen-tle. His touch sought out the least, the last and the lonely. His message was that if we are to walk in his footsteps we too must reach out and touch those who are in need.

During Advent we continue in the Irish tradition of monastic hospitality where the marginalised were welcomed. Hospitality was often very much in the tradition of the story of the widow's mite. Although they had very little to offer they gave generously, sharing the view of St Vincent de Paul who used to say to those who wanted to join his congregation: 'Never forget, my children, that the poor are our masters. That is why we should love them and serve them, with utter respect, and do what they bid us.'

We should serve those in need this Advent like they were Jesus. God can work through nothings, small things like us. He uses us to do his work. Over this Advent God, the suffering Jesus, will present himself to us in many, many forms. In our rush to prepare for Christmas we may miss him. How ironic would that be?

PRAYER

Be near to us when we most need you,
and out of our sufferings bring us joy.
You promised that where two or three
are gathered in your name,
you would be in their midst.
This Advent answer our earnest prayers
and take us by the hand on the path of goodness.

❊ ❊ ❊

FRIDAY

'The Lord lifts up those who are bowed down.' (Ps 146:8)

Reflection: When a child is born

Inevitably we connect Advent and Christmas with the birth of a baby in a stable.

God was born as a baby to highlight that in our weakness we will find strength to live the Christian life. If we were strong enough to do everything ourselves we would not have needed Jesus in the first place.

In Advent we are reminded that the child born in a stable in Bethlehem for whom 'there was no room in the inn' still has the power to challenge contemporary society in a very powerful way. One of the most important truths of the Christian faith which Christmas embodies is the fact of God's trust in humanity. The Nativity highlights most starkly the full measure of human responsibility and human destiny as it is a declaration of God's trust in humankind. The unknown God who is lord of all discloses to people that if they want to know what he is like, they should look in the stable – at a human life. This reminds us that us that God is a living God, someone who loves people and loves to be loved by people.

The baby came as, 'the way, the truth and the life'. He came to bring the Good News to the poor. It was a particular kind of Good News because its truth hurts as much as it liberates. Sadly there are many cosy corners that need to be challenged and many aspects of society that stand in need of liberation. I like to think also that especially at Advent and Christmas, with those for whom there is no one to share their rooms is Jesus. The sad reality is that life is difficult for many people. The message of Advent and Christmas is that Christ is made flesh not in the unreal beauty of the Christmas card but in the poor of our world. For those of us who claim to be Christian, Christ is made flesh in the poor.

What we celebrate at this time of the year is a simple but profound truth: God so loved the world that he sent us the greatest gift of all: his only Son to save us. Other religions speak of the divinisation of humanity. We celebrate the humanisation of God.

The birth of a baby put a smile on the face of the world. This baby comes with a call to all of us to serve. This season of Advent we can be a bridge between those who have and those who have less.

St Francis of Assisi wrote:
Let the whole of humankind tremble . . .
That the Lord of the universe, God and the Son of God,
so humbles Himself that for our salvation
He hides Himself under the little form of bread!
(*The Writings of St Francis of Assisi, translated by Paschal Robinson, 1905*)

Let us find Jesus this Advent.

Let us seek Jesus at the Lord's table this Christmas as we gather together rich and poor.

PRAYER

This Advent may we find God the Father.
This Advent may we find God the Son.
This Advent may we find God the Spirit.
May our love shine in every house.
May our love shine for those with no house.
May our love shine around every table.
May our love bring everybody to the table.

✿ ✿ ✿

SATURDAY

'You know the time has come: you must wake up now:
our salvation is even nearer than it was when we were
converted. The night is almost over, it will be daylight
soon let us give up all the things we prefer to do under
cover of the dark; let us arm ourselves and appear in
the light. Let your armour be the Lord Jesus Christ;

*forget about satisfying your bodies with all
their cravings.' (Rms 13:11–14)*

Reflection: Sing a Song of Joy

When I was a small boy every year at the end of the first week of the Advent season at school we started learning Christmas carols. Our teacher always started by reminding us that to sing was to praise God twice. As I had not been blessed with a singing voice, I found the repeated singing of these songs nothing less than an endurance test. However, there were lines from individual carols which penetrated my brain, highlighting the catechetical value of these songs. The line that struck me most forcibly was one from 'The Little Drummer Boy' ' . . . and he smiled at me'. The idea that Jesus was smiling at me stressed my dignity and value in God's eyes more eloquently than any sermon could have done.

Two lines from 'Little Town' also set me thinking.
'How silently, how silently,
the wondrous gift is given.'
The image of God that came to me because of these lyrics was of a shy God; not someone who wanted to be in the limelight but someone who was more comfortable in the background. Somehow I found that an attractive quality.

The mood of 'Joy to the World' was very inspiring and evocative. The picture that came to mind listening to that song was of a dancing God, rejoicing at the happiness of humankind, even if it was only a temporary affair.

However, the message of the song is that this not a season for magic. All our problems will not melt away. Rather the birth of a baby in a stable will create a new reality which will give us the strength to face up to the harsh aspects of modern life, to experience and to transmit the touch of God's gentle love. The message of the song is not that we get a ladder to climb up to heaven but instead that we have joy because God has come down from heaven to raise us up to new heights.

In the story of God's people in the Bible, when times were very bad and people were afraid or downhearted, the prophets taught them the value of turning to God in prayer. They spoke words of great hope because they believed that if we made time for God in our lives then we would learn to see things differently and to become strong in ourselves.

During this season, which is one of hope as we look forward to the birth of Christ, may we learn to place our trust in God who never leaves us or abandons us. May we be open to learning from all our experiences and come to understand that God speaks to us through all the events of our lives, be they good or bad. In this way we can face the future with confidence knowing that God will give us what we need for each day.

PRAYER
Lord,
May your energy explode within me,
for you are the author of all life.
Even your words breathe new life,
give me your life this Advent,
so that I may surrender to your love.
Set me free so that I may bring you glory.

❄ ❄ ❄

WEEK THREE

SUNDAY

*'Surely God is my salvation; I will trust, and will not
be afraid, for the Lord God is my strength and my
might; he has become my salvation.
With joy you will draw water from
the wells of salvation.
And you will say in that day: Give thanks to the
Lord, call on his name; make known his deeds among
the nations; proclaim that his name is exalted.
Sing praises to the Lord, for he has done gloriously;
let this be known in all the earth.
Shout aloud and sing for joy, O royal Jerusalem, for
great in your midst is the living God.*
(Is 12:2–6)

Reflection: A Time of Hope

These are difficult times to speak about hope. However, it is an interesting fact that in Spanish, (and also in French and Italian) the verb to hope can be translated into English as three different words. The verb *esperar* in Spanish can mean to hope, to wait for or to expect. That little piece of trivia gives us something to think about when it comes to reflecting on the season of Advent. It is traditionally presented as a time of waiting and that gives rise to a problem in our culture where waiting is almost universally seen as something negative. There is a widely held belief, promoted very effectively by a whole range of marketing executives, that we can have whatever we want whenever we want it. So why on earth would you wait?

The season of Advent offers a different perspective and that makes it important for our time. It suggests that some things are worth waiting for and that the very act of waiting helps to nourish in us a sense of expectancy and of hope. The waiting that Advent promotes is based on a trust that we will not be disappointed because what we are waiting on, hoping for and expecting is nothing less than God.

The prayers and readings of Advent invite us to take the time to reflect on what it is we are waiting for God to do. The people who assist us in this process are characters such as Isaiah an old prophet, John the Baptist, a young prophet and Mary, a pregnant teenager. Each in their turn is creative and imaginative, challenging and trusting and they are all people of prayer. Isaiah dared to dream that deserts might be turned into fertile plains, that the blind might see and the deaf might hear. John the Baptist dared to challenge his contemporaries that they needed to think and behave differently if they wanted a better world and Mary of Nazareth dared to believe that God could act through her simple yes to bring a light to the people who sat in darkness. The reason we look to these heroes of hope and expectation is not that we are interested in events of two millennia ago but that we learn from them what to hope for and expect from God now, at this time in our world. We learn from them that when we make gods in our image and likeness, we will be disappointed. They teach us that the key is to let God be God and then transformation occurs. This however requires a prayerful waiting and that does not come easily to us in our instant age. The advertisers would have us jump straight to Christmas, but if we want Christmas to mean something then we need to spend a little time with Isaiah, John and Mary.

PRAYER

Lord, may our faith and trust in
you become deeper this Advent.
Lord, speak to our hearts.
Lord, you were born poor among the poor,
may our hearts always be open to those in need.
Lord, speak to our hearts.
Lord, teach us to recognise the many
blessings we have and to say thanks.
Lord speak to our hearts.

❋ ❋ ❋

Monday

*'For surely I know the plans I have for you, says the
Lord, plans for your welfare and not for harm,
to give you a future with hope.
Then when you call upon me and come and
pray to me, I will hear you.
When you search for me, you will find me; if you
seek me with all your heart, I will let you find me, says
the Lord, and I will restore you and bring you back to
myself.' (Jer 29:10–11)*

Reflection: In the beginning was the Word
As a boy I learned a story which always return to me every Advent. Sometimes the simplicity of a child's story hides a

deep truth, as I hope this tale illustrates.

God created the heavens and the earth and everything in them. Words were his creative agents because words are power. God spoke: 'Let it be done' and it was done. And everything he made was good.

The apple of God's eye was the man and woman he created because he had breathed into them a part of himself, his spirit. The countryside smelled clean and fresh, and the scent of soil mingled with the heavier odour of grass and fresh vegetation. The man and the woman followed a road that took them through a wood, and some of its trees seemed to have been there before time even began, they were so gnarled and ancient. A brook accompanied them most of the way, trickling between its muddy banks with a gentle bubbling sound. Beautiful blackbirds sang from the top branch of the tall oak trees, and a dog barked with pleasure in the distance. The devil was jealous that God had partners to share his love and vowed to teach him a lesson. One day when God was chatting with Adam and Eve the devil sneaked up behind him and put a bond on his tongue so that he could not speak. God could no longer talk and because his creative power was in his words, the devil had denied him that power. It was not raining, but the clouds were low and menacing and it was crystal clear that a deluge was coming. The man and woman were astonished and closed their eyes in apparent despair.

The devil made fun of God and kept him in captivity for a long time. Every hour the devil would return to taunt him. Eventually God responded by waving one finger. Intrigued the devil asked him if he wanted to say just one word. God nodded a definite yes.

The devil thought to himself 'sure one word can do no

harm' and removed the bond. Adam and Eve, pale and heavy-eyed, said nothing. God had a gleam in his eye that said he was looking forward to outwitting his enemies. He spoke one word in a whisper so gentle that the devil could barely hear him. The word released all the forgiveness that God had been storing in his heart during his period of silence. Dawn came early, with streaks of pale blue sky showing through the clouds.

The devil tugged his cloak around him as if he suddenly found the garden too cold and squawked as icy water seeped into his boots, and then he released a string of vulgar words. His face was a mask of anger, furious that a single word should cause him so much misery. He exaggerated a shiver as he stood alone.

The word was **Jesus.**

PRAYER

Lord, may we learn to make time for prayer
and to discover just how close you are to us.
Lord help us to listen.
Lord, in our preparation for Christmas
remind us about what is really important.
Lord help us to listen.
Lord, may our love be sincere and not just
for those who love us.
Lord help us to listen.

❅ ❅ ❅

TUESDAY

*'And Mary said, "My soul magnifies the Lord, and
my spirit rejoices in God my Saviour, for he has looked
with favour on the lowliness of his servant. Surely,
from now on all generations will call me blessed; for
the Mighty One has done great things for me, and
holy is his name. His mercy is for those who revere
him from generation to generation. He has shown
strength with his arm; he has scattered the proud in
the thoughts of their hearts. He has brought down the
powerful from their thrones and lifted up the lowly;
he has filled the hungry with good things and sent the
rich away empty.' (Lk 1:46–53)*

Reflection: Star of the Sea

Traditionally in Ireland we welcomed the fine weather
by joining the rush to erect a May altar in honour of Our
Lady. Flowers were piled into jam jars for decorations. The
most colourful ceremony of all was the procession from
the chapel down to the village. It seemed to be an injunc-
tion for the sacred to leave the church and make its home
in the ordinary. Every house along the way was decorated
with flowers. From an early age we were given a great de-
votion for the Virgin Mary, Intercessor, Mother of Mercy,
Star of the Sea. To call upon the father for daily bread and
praise the kingdom, the power and the glory was inspiring and comforting but we felt a warm glow within us
when we spoke phrases like 'fruit of thy womb.'

Mary was an integral part of the fabric of Irish life, even
Irish history. One story I learned as a boy was about the
Virgin Mary walking by a house in the West of Ireland

on a stormy night during the Great Famine. She and the child Jesus had no coat to protect them from the elements. As they passed the house, the woman of the house called them inside and gave Mary a bowl of nettle soup, and an old sack to give extra cover to the child. Mary's final blessing was that the family line would always remain intact. They were one of the few families who survived the Great Hunger. A sign that God's favour rested on them was that their rooster did not crow 'cockadoodledoo' but rather cried out: 'the Virgin's Son is risen'.

Advent is a good time for remembering how much we can learn from Mary, the mother of Jesus. We can learn from her words like those in her prayer, the Magnificat. These are words of joy and praise from a girl who, on the face of it, did not have much to be joyful about. However, she was willing to believe that God was working in and through her to bring about remarkable change in the world. She also believed that God wanted to do the same in us. So later when her child had grown up she spoke to us and said, 'Do whatever he tells you'. In the story of Christmas she is presented as not saying too much but as simply 'pondering these things in her heart'. We can learn from her attitude to her life and what was going on in it. She knew the value of reflecting and would continue to do this even to the end when she stood by her son's cross.

PRAYER

Lord, in the person of Mary you teach how
us to be open to your Holy Spirit.
Lord may we be willing to learn.
Lord, in the person of Mary you teach us
how to place our trust in you.

Lord may we be willing to learn.
Lord, in the person of Mary you teach
us how to give thanks.
Lord may we be willing to learn.
Lord, in the person of Mary you teach us how
to be faithful to your son
Lord may we be willing to learn.

✿ ✿ ✿

WEDNESDAY

*'And the angel said to them, "Fear not, for behold, I
bring you good news of great joy that will be for all the
people. For unto you is born this day in the city of
David a Saviour, who is Christ the Lord".'*
(Lk 2:10–11)

Reflection: I Have a Dream

Jesus had a dream. His dream was God's dream. He
dreamt that all people would live together as one family,
God's family. Jesus dreamt of a world where no one would
be hungry and have nothing to eat, where no one would
be thirsty and have nothing to drink, where no one would
be naked and have nothing to wear, where no one would
be sick and have no one to visit them, where no one would
be in prison and rejected by their community (Mt 25). Jesus
dreamt that all people would love each other, care for each
other, share with each other and respect each other. What
unites us as Christians is that we share this dream of Jesus.

To follow Jesus is to announce to the world that we have
committed our lives to building this dream for all of us to
live together as God's precious people.

God's dream, God's hope for our world then, is that we might love one another as God has loved us, by reaching out to those who suffer: the poor, the homeless, the lonely, the sick, the rejected and the unwanted. Jesus came to make God's dream for our world a reality. To transform our world from where it is today to where God would like it to be tomorrow requires a revolution. That revolution is the community of Christians, which Jesus called the Kingdom of God.

Advent is a time to reconnect ourselves with this dream of Jesus and to make the change of heart that is required.

This dream brings with it all the hopes and challenges of any new beginning. Every year certainly brings more than its share of difficulties and many of these will be with us for the foreseeable future. So as we head into this New Year where are the sources of hope?

They lie, as always, in the people whose lives continue to demonstrate the remarkable resilience of the human spirit: the dedicated teachers who, on a daily basis, give their best and inspire countless young people to do the same; the young people who cope with all the turbulence of their teen years and yet manage to find great freedom and joy in the gradual discovery of their gifts and talents, and who show the value of friendship in so many ways.

In short, the sources of hope are all around us in the members of our communities, the people, who go about their work with commitment and good humour always with an eye to caring for those who might be finding things difficult. So let us begin the new year as we mean to go on: let us never underestimate the faith, love and generosity of those around us, let us not be slow to smile and say thanks and let us always try to give our best, trusting that there is a power greater than us at work to bring about the good.

PRAYER
Lord,
We celebrate this season not because
of the rising of the sun,
but because of the birth of the Son.
In this great season,
We await your promise
That true peace has come down from heaven:
the beginning of a new era of redemption,
the deliverance announced of old,
of eternal happiness and unending joy.

❁ ❁ ❁

THURSDAY

'So stay awake, because you do not know the day when the master is coming. You may be quite sure of this that if the householder had known at what time of the night the burglar would come, he would have stayed awake and would not have allowed anyone to break through the wall of his house. Therefore, you too must stand ready because the Son of Man is coming at an hour you do not expect.' (Mt 24:42–44)

Reflection: Learning for a Reason
Some old customs can momentarily transfigure our existence and let the eternal shine through. One such custom we had as children was the singing of carols. They also struck me as simple ways of expressing those parts of

Christianity that ordinary people found most interesting, not the parts that people *ought* to find most interesting. They were memorable because they were so tangible. They celebrated things that we could touch and see and warm to: a mother and a baby, and a foster-father (although that exact language might not have been used at the time), a stable, donkeys, shepherds, straw and hay. The miracle they celebrated was the making of an all-powerful God, child sized, so that even the youngest infant could grasp what it was all about. More importantly, they reminded us of the happy character of our faith, that Christianity was a reason for rejoicing. God became small for the sole purpose of saving us all. This was part of the beauty of the festive season where past and future meet in the present.

Learning these carols did have a practical value because we could sing them on Wren Boys' Day. On St Stephen's Day we dressed up in old clothes with lines of lipstick on our faces and cycled to all the houses for miles around, where we sang, or more often wailed, in the confident expectation that we would be rewarded with a few coins for our musical offering. Motley groups appeared on the roads or laneways looking like gangs of tramps in their assorted rags, faces masked or blackened. They did a jig or reel or sang a song, trying to disguise their voices, clinking the coins in their collection tins, chorused their thanks and were on the way to make more money. Our motivation was purely mercenary, but the carols did help us in a small way to comprehend a mystery we could only dimly understand.

The one song I performed every year that was not a carol was John Lennon's 'And so This is Christmas'. It is a magical song because it is really an anthem especially the line 'War is Over'. It was a great song to be singing again and again because it helped me to link the coming of the son with peace. This child's vision was for a world where we all stood shoulder-to-shoulder with one another and commit ourselves to justice and peace for the good of all. Thus we can be a blessing to one another and the world.

Advent is a time when we make a particular effort to be a blessing to the world.

PRAYER
Lord,
I want you to be my constant companion,
because only you can meet my needs.
Be at my side at every waking moment,
may your presence be ever present to me.
Stay close at my moments of crisis,
when it seems as if I am losing control.

✿ ✿ ✿

FRIDAY

*'God of hosts, turn again, we implore,
look down from heaven and see.
visit this vine and protect it,
the vine your right hand has planted.'(Ps 79:15–16)*

Reflection: Do you Know It's Nearly Christmas?
Advent is a time for us to embrace the uplifting words of Pope Francis: 'We love this beautiful planet on which God has put us, and we love the human family which dwells here, with all its tragedies and struggles, its hopes and aspirations, its strengths and weaknesses. The earth is

our common home and all of us are brothers and sisters.' (Pope Francis, *Evangelii Gaudium*)

Pope Francis is reminding us that if we are to share our lives with others and generously give of ourselves, we also have to realise that every person is worthy of our giving – not for their physical appearance, their abilities, their language, their way of thinking or for any satisfaction that we might receive, but rather because they are God's handiwork, an essential part of the fabric and tapestry of the divine creation.

This is a lovely ideal. Sadly it is not the reality. If Pope Francis is to see his dream fulfilled we are all challenged to prepare to build a new reality and a new world – which owes more to the values of Jesus than to the values of the marketplace. We must prepare to make the kingdom come.

Preparation is an essential part of everyday living. We prepare for different things in different ways. If an important event is about to happen in our lives we usually put a lot of preparation. The amount of preparation we invest in something gives a good indication of how highly we value it in our lives. The weeks before Christmas are always a time of preparation, sending cards, buying presents and food. Advent is a time when we prepare for the coming of Christ. It is a time of joy, a time of hope but also a time of self-examination. Advent is a time for asking ourselves a very fundamental question: what is the meaning of God's presence in my life? At the Annunciation, God asked Mary the question: 'Will you bring Christ into the world?' Mary's answer was yes. Gently Christ entered the world, entered our lives. Like us she asked, 'what is the meaning of God's presence in my life?' Today we are faced with the question as Mary: 'Will you bring Christ into the world'?

Saying yes to that question means taking a real step in faith, because we do not know the full meaning of our yes. This will not unfold as we go along. But just as Mary felt the child grow within her and joyfully received him on the day of his birth, so we will also discover that in our darkness, he is there – just as he has been all along.

PRAYER
Lord,
When I feel most empty and vulnerable,
you raise me up with tender hands.
My security is in your promise of eternal friendship,
and the knowledge that you will never let go of me.
As I look to your second coming,
shower me with your love.
May I be a messenger of your Advent.

❄ ❄ ❄

SATURDAY

*'May the Lord be generous in increasing your love
and make you love one another and the whole human
race as much as we love you. And may he so confirm
your hearts in holiness that you may be blameless in
the sight of our God and father when our Lord Jesus
Christ comes with all his saints.'*
(Thess 3:12–4:1)

Reflection: Have Courage
One Christmas there was a young prince who was meandering around distant lands looking for adventure. One morning in December he had opened a window shutter and watched dawn steal across the fields. The sky turned

from black to dark blue, then to violet. The landscape became full of grey shadows, which gradually resolved into trees, hedges, fences and buildings. There was no sign of the sun, hidden as it was behind a layer of cloud, but the prince felt better that the night was over.

He came to a town that was near a pass into a fertile valley as he was thinking about the mysteries that confronted him. He had arrived just as the Christmas service was finishing and most of the congregation were leaving in a rush, eager to begin their Christmas festivities and enjoy their Christmas meals.

Nonetheless the prince was taken aback by the poverty in the town and inquired why the people did not move into the valley. The locals told him that they couldn't because a dragon was guarding the pass and that they were all afraid of him. The prince sighed, and the townsfolk saw lines of weariness etched into his face.

The prince decided that he was going to solve the problem irrespective of his own personal safety. With a brave smile but with a knot in his stomach the prince made his way to the pass. It was accessed by a wooden bridge so dangerously ruinous that crossing the moat was an adventure in itself. The prince frowned a little but took it in his stride. With his sword waving he reached his destination. He rubbed a hand through his fine hair, feeling his stomach tie itself in knots. To his great surprise all he could see was a tiny little dragon, who only was the size of his boot.

'Where's your father?' asked the prince, his voice loud and full of self-importance. The dragon stepped forward to make a low and very sincere obeisance and said, 'I live here on my own'.

'But how can a tiny little beast like you so terrify the

local people?', trying to keep the reproach from his voice but not succeeding.

'Because of my name'.

'What's your name?'

'What Might Happen?'

It is said that courage is not the absence of fear but rather the judgement that something else is more important than fear. If we turn away from a challenge once, it is so much easier to do the same again the next time, and the next. Showing some courage in less serious difficulties is often the best training for the major crises. Courage is like a muscle. It is strengthened with use.

Advent is a time to let go of any foolish fears.

PRAYER

Lord,
because I want you to take over my life.
In you I shall find wholeness,
a source of vision and virtue.
There are moments when I am more
conscious of your absence,
than finding glory in your presence.
Help me to find you again.

✵ ✵ ✵

Week Four

Sunday

'In the sixth month the angel Gabriel was sent by God to a town in Galilee called Nazareth, to a virgin betrothed to a man named Joseph, of the House of David; and the virgin's name was Mary. He went in and said her, ''Rejoice, so highly favoured! The Lord is with you''.' (Lk 1:26–38)

Reflection: Rejoice O Highly Favoured

Growing up on a farm I never failed to get a little thrill from bringing a lamb into the world, especially after a very difficult birth. I felt I was part in some small way of achieving the miracle of new life. It would be melodramatic to say it was a religious experience but a warmth flowed through my body. The birth was a language of hope, lyrical, alive to the resonances of everyday life. The first sound of the breathing of the new lamb was the breathing of hope.

   Life on a farm is always surrounded by the presence of hope. There is a colour and a shape that constantly resists that which is too clear. It always surprises and offers new vistas where wisdom and welcome conspire. It is constantly ready to dispense opportunities to enhance our life experience. Farming can reach deep into the world that lives within us. Each new day can be a new beginning, a gift from God full of creativity and feeling, investing all our energies in an environment where our souls and intellects are fully engaged in the fresh air of God's glorious creation.

Now that I live in the city I understand that all forms of human life are gifts. Everything in our lives is intended by God as a gift to us. Jesus was God's ultimate gift. Throughout his human life he gloried in the gift of life, the gift of nature and above all the gift of people. Mary's life too was a gift of God to us.

While Mary was honoured with the greatest gift of all she also had her own trials and tribulations. She received the Good News at the Annunciation but she also had to watch her son suffer in agony on the cross at Calvary. Her gifts were matched by her crosses. In this way she is close to our own lives – which are unique mixtures of joy and sadness.

After the initial joy of her conception subsided she had to wait for the birth of her baby. As time went by she realised that many would claim her as yet unborn baby and eventually take him from her. It is difficult to carry a child for nine months with that thought in your mind. Mary was preparing herself for both joy and sorrow.

She wondered and reflected as she nurtured the child growing within her. We often think of Mary as different from ourselves but, reflecting on her life, we discover that she herself walked in darkness and uncertainty before us. She herself has known our fears and insecurities. That is why we can turn to her with confidence in our moments of crisis.

PRAYER
Mary,
Source of comfort in every age,
you conceived and bore your son,
who is known as the Prince of Peace.
Blessed are you above all other women
and hallowed is the fruit of your womb,
for you conceived the Christ, the Son
and have redeemed our souls.

✤ ✤ ✤

MONDAY

'A shoot springs from the stock of Jesse,
a scion thrusts from his roots:
on him the spirit of the Lord rests,
a spirit of wisdom and insight,
a spirit of counsel and power,
a spirit of knowledge and the fear of the Lord.' (Is 11:1–2)

Reflection: Bringing Light to Darkness

Let me not to the marriage of true minds
Admit impediments. Love is not love
Which alters when it alteration finds …
(William Shakespeare Sonnet 116)

The mystery of love is at the heart of the spirituality of Advent, a life of self-giving, of dying to one's selfishness and being for others. Our baptism invites us into the paschal mystery, the dying and rising Jesus witnessed for us. Being 'for' and 'with' others in their need fulfils the Lord's basic commandment.

Shakespeare's insight for us this Advent is that authentic love does not alter or admit of impediments. We witness this type of love in a spouse who continues to visit daily, even for years, a married partner with dementia to take just one example. The marital love is not diminished, even though the sick partner is unable to communicate. It is amazing grace which lights up the Advent season.

Throughout his plays and sonnets, Shakespeare offers nuggets of advice for us Advent pilgrims. In *The Merchant of Venice*, we listen attentively to Portia: 'So shines a good deed in a naughty world' (Act 5, Scene 1). One act of kindness can transform a life.

In the build-up to Christmas people are raising money for a whole range of worthy projects from Christmas Shoeboxes for needy children to fundraisers for St Vincent de Paul. Carollers sing on the streets, cake sales and toy fares are held by the score and school children arrange a proliferation of food collections. It is a timely reminder of the needs of the human community.

Everywhere we look we see the tragic face of human suffering. The plight of these people presents problems for belief in God, particularly a God who apparently sits back and allows people to destroy themselves. How can we survive as credible witnesses to the God of love, to the God of history, to the God of creation and power? It raises problems for our view of a loving and powerful God taking care of his own. What kind of God can leave people to wallow in suffering?

Yet such a judgement is totally unfair. The best answer to this charge is provided by Elie Wiesel's book *Night*. He was trying to answer the difficult question why did God allow the ghastly nightmare of the Holocaust. Walking through the concentration camp he sees a young boy being hanged and reflects:

'Behind me I heard the same man asking, ''Where is God now?'' And I heard a voice within me answer him, ''Where is he? Here he is. He is hanging there on this gallows.'' That night the soup tasted of corpses.'

It is somewhere in the heart of the darkness that we find both the God of the Jews and the God of Jesus. It is somewhere there, taking on humankind's evil, suffering with the victims of humankind's inhumanity to people, that our God is to be found. This is the God who is revealed to us out of the darkness. This is the God who is waiting for us this Advent.

PRAYER
Lord,
As you were born in a stable in Bethlehem,
be born again in my spirit.
Let me live by justice
and with goodness and mercy.
Renew my flickering hope
because your mercy is here
your time and our time has come at last.

❅ ❅ ❅

TUESDAY

'What we are waiting for is what he promised: the new heavens and new earth, the place where righteousness will be at home. So then, my friends, while you are waiting, do your best to live lives without spot or stain so that he will find you at peace.' (2 Pet 3:13–14)

Reflection: God's Earthly Ambassador

St John's Gospel announces with a flourish: 'And the Word was made flesh . . . ' With one fell swoop we learn from this dramatic and almost incomprehensible revelation of the immense love of God. The Incarnation turned the ways of the world on its head. After this event glory is to be found in humiliation, riches in poverty and, most strangely of all, life in death.

It is for this reason that St Paul can say that the Word came in the flesh of sin, under the law, like a slave, and under the power of death. His 'failure' and final humiliation began the moment he was received by Mary at the cross.

God wanted to take on a human form so that we might find him in others. The tragic parts of our human existence, our poverty and weakness, our sickness, darkness and death have all being graced by the presence of God. All the darkest forces of the human condition are now basically filled with the truth of his life, with his freedom that is authentic freedom, with the majesty of his power. We do not have to seek God any more in the heavens. He is right here amongst us. He is sharing our burden, has tasted the bitterness of our life, has travelled our highways and byways.

Through the incarnation a new force and spirit has entered the world – light, love, wisdom and joy has entered the human heart and mind, and in the eyes of God, a new springtime has begun in all of creation. The prophets had been telling about his coming. The world has waited generations for this day. From Mary's humanity, she gave him his humanity. Every heartbeat of hers gave him a heart to love with. The ordinary has become the extraordinary and the extraordinary has become ordinary.

During the special season we marvel at the miraculous. The crucified Jesus has unexpectedly become the risen Christ. The eternal has invaded the transient. The Jesus of Good Friday has shown once for all that God's relationship with each of us transcends the limitations of this life. This was his 'Good News' to the poor, a kingdom in which the excluded are brought in, the blind are given sight, the paralysed walk and sinners are forgiven.

Advent is the time we are given the breathing space to prepare for the real presence. It is a gentle call to slow down and reflect on the bigger picture. Who is the God of the Paschal Mystery for us today?

This is a time when more than any other we are aware of the life that makes us live, the expectation of a new beginning, new birth and hope and the inexhaustible, now accessible divine potential that is all around us. It is a welcome opportunity to savour the energy, joy and trust of the unique Christmas laughter.

PRAYER

Mary,
We think of you today
and remember your journey to the stable,
where you gave birth to the Saviour.
We rejoice on this wondrous occasion
and we worship him who chose to become
a new-born baby,
while remaining God in all eternity.

✻ ✻ ✻

WEDNESDAY

'Jerusalem, take off your dress of sorrow and distress,
put on the beauty of the glory of God for ever, wrap the
cloak of the integrity of God around you.' (Bar 5:1)

Reflection: The Giving of the Magi

This special season of Advent Jesus, the Word made flesh, makes it clear that God's only desire for us is that we should have life and to have it to the full. In response we ask God to give us the grace to trust ourselves to the Father and to live accordingly.

As a child the Sunday before Christmas was always the day for setting up the crib. This task was conducted with an air of great solemnity. My job always was to look after the three characters who represented the Magi.

The crib gave me a great insight into the minds and hearts of the characters of the first Christmas. The story was old yet new each year. I never failed to wonder at the wonderful, how God took time to enter human history. The baby's life was one of contradiction even at birth because a young girl, still a virgin gave him life. His birth was so significant that even the stars were thrown into rapture and subservience. An infant's voice was turning the world on its head. He was only different in seeing evil but not part of it.

I am not sure if it represented good liturgical practice to include the three wise men in the crib, yet it did help me to associate giving with wisdom. When the Magi brought gifts to the babe in the manger they invented the art of giving presents at Christmas. I noted the significance of Christ coming as the greatest gift of all but also receiving gifts. This suggested that love is about receiving as well as giving. To have one without the other diminishes its power and leaves a gap in the lives of those who wish to participate in it.

This was a welcome corrective to the warped understanding of Christian love I had assimilated, as something we 'do' for others. The enormity of meaning in the incarnation is almost mind-blowing, yet, the crib did help me to understand a simple but profound truth. Jesus came and made himself small, so that we could be raised to heights we could not dared to have dreamed of otherwise.

PRAYER
Father,
In this child we see in Bethlehem,
we know that your promises are true.
You gave us no less than your very self,
so that we may be ever more yours.
You did not send him as a king,
to be exalted among the great,
but to serve us, to be born,
to live and to die for us.

❀ ❀ ❀

THURSDAY

'So Joseph set out from the town of Nazareth in Galilee and travelled up to Judea, to the town of David called Bethlehem, since he was of David's House and line, in order to be registered together with Mary, his betrothed, who was with child. While they were there the time came for her to have the child, and she gave birth to her son, her first born.' (Lk 2:2–6)

Reflection: The Origin of the Christmas Species

Traditionally it was the custom on the evening of Christmas Eve to request the youngest child of a household to light a candle, which was then placed in the window. This little light of the household twinkled in answer to the brightest star in the sky which, the children were informed, was the same star which shone in Bethlehem on the night that Jesus was born. And thus the two worlds – this earth below and heaven above – were united at the sacred time.

Today Scripture scholars believe that Jesus Christ in all probability was born about the year which we designated as 4BC and that he was put to death by the Roman procurator in AD29. Neither the Gospels nor any other sources give the precise date of his birth, however, and indeed it was not until the fourth century that the Church decided on a special day in the year on which to celebrate the nativity of its founder.

The day selected was 25 December, no doubt in large measure to replace the old pagan Roman feast but with a sound theological foundation because Christ was the definitive 'light of the world' and his coming on earth was the beginning of a new era.

In the tough winter climate that date had special symbolic force, symbolising the hope inherent in the Gospel narrative of how a saviour was born out of the very circumstances of degradation – in a stable amongst animals and without a roof over his head.

Life may be compared to a journey and along the way we learn from others who have gone ahead of us and whose experience can speak to us.

We also learn from those who walk with us, sharing the road. As people of faith we trust that we are not alone on this journey and that, in fact, our closest companion is Jesus who has not only gone ahead of us but also still walks with us.

For many centuries now people have meditated on the journey that Jesus made beginning in a stable in Bethlehem and from that they have learned much about him and about themselves. They feel encouraged to go on, to continue even when things are difficult and darkness threatens to drag them down. Jesus, the great teacher, gives remarkable lessons on courage and commitment, love and compassion, generosity and hope. These are some of the reasons why people all over the world still try to walk the way of Jesus in Advent. The potential of this message remains ever new in the Christian tradition. At the heart of the widespread appeal of Christianity is the belief that the last shall be first and the first last.

PRAYER
Lord,
You gave up your own life,
such was the extent of your generosity.
How can we thank you enough?
You came and made all things new.
You bring new life to all.
Help us to bring new life this season.

❄ ❄ ❄

FRIDAY

*While they were there, the time came for her to deliver
her child. And she gave birth to her firstborn son
and wrapped him in bands of cloth, and laid him in
a manger, because there was no place for them in the
inn. In that region there were shepherds living in the
fields, keeping watch over their flock by night. Then an
angel of the Lord stood before them, and the glory of
the Lord shone around them, and they were terrified.
But the angel said to them, "Do not be afraid; for see
I am bringing you good news of great joy for all the
people: to you is born this day in the city of David a
Saviour, who is the Messiah, the Lord. This will be a
sign for you: you will find a child wrapped in bands
of cloth and lying in a manger." And suddenly there
was with the angel a multitude of the heavenly host,
praising God and saying: "Glory to God in the
highest heaven, and on earth peace among
those whom he favours!"' (Lk 2:6–14)*

Reflection: It's part of who we are

*And is it true? And is it true,
This most tremendous tale of all,
Seen in a stained-glass window's hue,
A Baby in an ox's stall?
The Maker of the stars and sea
Become a Child on earth for me?*

(Sir John Betjeman 'Christmas' from *A Few Late Chrysanthemums*)

The poet gets to the heart of the matter in this simple poem
about Christmas. He asks a key question: can it be true that

the child in the manger is God? If this is so, and as Catholic Christians we say that it is, then all human life is changed and every human being receives a dignity and value beyond our wildest imaginings. Christmas becomes a feast of hope and incredible joy and it would be very sad if we were to lose sight of that. Of course it is good to party with family and friends and to exchange gifts. It is great to have a bit of fun to get us over the mid-winter blues. But Christmas is about much more than that. Our history gives us an important clue in this respect. Celtic Christianity was literally down to earth. It had no sense of rigid dichotomy between the secular and the sacred. The Gaelic language ensured that the most mundane of social intercourse became occasions of prayer. In the Celtic tradition people are blessed every time they say goodbye in the phrase, '*Go mbeannaí Dia dhuit*' (God bless you). The standard greeting to friend and stranger was, '*Dia is Muire dhíbh*'. (God and Mary be with you). What is particularly instructive is that many of these greetings are in the plural as the presence of Christ in the other is also acknowledged.

God was understood as appreciative of and protective of every single human life. The Celtic description of a disabled person as God's own person (*duine le Dia*) is a good illustration of that point. In the Celtic tradition old life, injured life, disabled life: every life is God's own life, God's special gift and task. Advent is a golden opportunity for us to learn about our heritage as Irish people and as Christians and to make everyone feel valued.

PRAYER

Lord, creator of all that is, you come
among us as a human being
May our celebration of Christmas be blessed.
Lord you come among us to make
the world a better place
May our celebration of Christmas be blessed,
Lord, you come among us to teach us the way of love
May our celebration of Christmas be blessed.

✿ ✿ ✿

SATURDAY

*'She wrapped him in swaddling clothes and laid him in
a manager because there was no room for them at the
inn. In the countryside close by there were shepherds
who lived in the fields and took it in turns to watch
their flocks during the night. The angel of the Lord
shone around them. They were terrified, but the angel
said, ''Do not be afraid. Listen, I bring you news of
great joy, a joy to be shared by the whole people''.'*
(Lk 2:11–13)

Reflection: The Saviour's Day

John Lennon wrote a beautiful Christmas song which asks
us to recall that it is Christmas and as another year is over
we should ask: what have we done?

He wrote another called 'Imagine'. Who could not be
captivated by his dream of a world at peace? Maybe we
could add a verse: imagine a world where people forgive
each other and never seek revenge. For many that is just
wishful thinking. For Jesus it was how he lived and died.

Forgiveness is hard work and at times it seems impossible. So we needed someone to help us understand that it is, in the first place, not something we do but something we receive; it is a gift from God who loves us totally. Maybe then we will be able to forgive others as God has forgiven us. That is why God became a baby.

At Midnight Mass as a child there was always a crush of people. The attendance was swelled by immigrants home from Christmas, a welcome respite for families divided by economic necessity. Christmas Eve was a time of delirious reunions as trains and buses to Athlone and Roscommon brought husbands, fathers, daughters, sons, girlfriends and boyfriends home to the bosom of their families.

The standard greeting of Mass-goers to one another was 'A Happy Christmas', their breath like plumed smoke in the frosty air. The final candle in the advent wreath was lit ceremoniously. So many of my images of Christ were etched in light, the silver of frost and moonlight, the shining Star of Bethlehem guarding the Magi and the radiance of the lighted candles.

The choir sang lustily. Then a solo rendering of 'O Holy Night' that was so beautiful it worked a minor miracle and hushed all the coughing and shuffling.

The focal point of the church was the crib, with a big silver star shining in the roof, and a little baby so real I would not have been surprised if he began to wail in his diminutive straw manger. It did at least remind me that it was a baby, not Santa Claus that was, is and always would be Christmas.

The Christmas of childhood no longer exists. I feel nostalgic about it and I miss a lot of it. So many facets of life are very different now. Yet, there is one constant about

Christmas. The clothes may be very different but for many people there are more smiles than usual.

That great theologian I mentioned at the start of the book, Karl Rahner, said a lot of complicated things about the Christian faith, but one thing he said that everybody can understand is that at Christmas God gives us permission to be happy.

Let us try to accept God's generous invitation.

PRAYER
Lord, you come among us to offer us forgiveness
May our celebration of Christmas be blessed.
Lord, you come among us to bring us peace
May our celebration of Christmas be blessed.
Lord, you come among us to give us joy
May our celebration of Christmas be blessed.

❄ ❄ ❄